The 7 Steps On How To Build A Lasting Relationship With Your Money: Lasting Relationships with Money, Leads to a Brighter Future

This book will provide you with the steps that you will need to both build, and maintain a lasting relationship with your money. Financial stability is the most important factor in the way we decide to spend our money. This book will show you how to respect every penny that you make, and simple ways to manage every penny that you spend. Once you have mastered each step, your money issues will be a thing of the past.

By

Victor E Smalls

The 7 Steps on How To Build A Lasting Relationship With Your Money:
Lasting Relationships with Money, Leads to a Brighter Future

By

Victor E Smalls

Cadmus Publishing
CadmusPublishing.com

The 7 Steps on How To Build A Lasting Relationship With Your Money:
Lasting Relationships with Money, Leads to a Brighter Future

Manufactured in the United States of America. Copyright 2025 by Victor E. Smalls. All rights reserved. No part of this book may be reproduced in any form, audio, digital, or in print, except excerpts by reviewers, without written permission from the copyright holder.

DISCLAIMER:
The thoughts, opinions, and expressions herein are those of the author. Any similarities to actual events or people are purely coincidental. Names and distinguishing characteristics may have been changed to preserve the identities of any individuals. Published by Victor E. Smalls.

ISBN# 978-1-63751-527-3

Book Catalog Info Categories:
Reference

Cadmus Publishing
CadmusPublishing.com

Special Thanks Section

I want to first thank God for guiding me into this path to help others, I want to thank my loving mother, brothers, sisters, nieces, and nephew, as well as all of my childhood friends, and newfound friends that helped me remain focused in life. I want to thank my childhood sweetheart and wife for sticking by me and believing in me, our loving family keeps me going. I want to thank the H.O.N.O.R. Program and the many facilitators, The Financial Empowerment Workshop shout-outs to Q, Sleep, and Uncle Paul your program inspired this book in many ways, and the entire H.O.N.O.R. Program community. I thank you all for creating and maintaining the therapeutic space needed for a project such as this book to be completed. Again I want to thank God Almighty for his everlasting faith in me.

TABLE OF CONTENTS

SPECIAL THANK'S..0
Chapter One: "Understanding Your Money"............1-7
Chapter Two: "Save Before You Spend"................8-18
Chapter Three: " Budgeting Your Money".............19-33
Chapter Four: "Avoiding a Fixed-Mindset Vs. Becoming One with the Growth-Mindset"............................. 34-40
Chapter Five: " Invest Into Your Own Vision's"...41-47
Chapter Six: "Prioritizing Needs Over Wants".... 48-54
Chapter Seven: " Reaping the Benefits of Your Money in the Long Run"..55-57
WORD'S OF MOTIVATION..58
WISE WORD'S FROM A GOOD BROTHER.............59

Chapter 1

Understanding Your Money

The 7 Steps on How To Build A Lasting Relationship With Your Money – Victor E. Smalls

"Understanding Your Money"

This chapter will help you gain a better understanding about your money. Money can either make you better off in the long run, or make you suffer in some form. The beautiful thing is that you are in sole control of the relationship that you decide to build with your money. So for those excessive spenders, the first step provided in this book will pull you out of that toxic relationship that you currently have with your money... The first way to understand money is by putting in the work to earn it. A person that earns their money is more likely to know the value of money. Knowing the value of money does not mean that you understand it or respect it. All this means is that you know that with this money one can pay for X or buy Z.

There are three main things to know about understanding money, and once you have mastered these then you can say that you understand money. The first thing is that money has no

The 7 Steps on How To Build A Lasting Relationship With Your Money – Victor E. Smalls

emotions, so it doesn't hurt anyone to put that money to work! Making your money work for you is the biggest tool in really understanding your money. No need to feel bad in doing this because your money's purpose is to make more of itself, and in the long run you will reap the benefits, trust me. One benefit, is in fact the second thing to know about money, which is that money can be very supportive. Yes, money is a key source within your support system. Unless you can sit back and think of ways to survive without money, please contact me because I would love that knowledge. Now the catch to making money supportive is that you find ways to make that money work for you. Before you can really make money work for you, it is vital to learn how to sacrifice. Once you sacrifice, you will see how the last main thing to know is how your money becomes more loyal to you when it's treated right. When you start making sacrifices in life as it relates to spending, you will see how loyal your money will become. Money has always been loyal to those who takes time to understand it.

THE MOST IMPORTANT THINGS TO REMEMBER ABOUT MONEY:

1. Money has no emotions
2. Money can be very supportive
3. Money becomes loyal when treated right

When you think about your money, just relate it to the perfect type of relationship. A relationship with money is one that we all should strive to maintain. The thing about money is that when it's treated right it will never let you down, nor will it ever stop supporting you. No matter how careless you are with money, once it's in your possession, the promise that money provides will never change. That promise is that money will make you better financially in the long run, as long as you commit to its overall growth.

Follow these steps and you will most certainly become more familiar with your money. Understanding money is the key to financial success. Most people know how to earn money, but only a

The 7 Steps on How To Build A Lasting Relationship With Your Money – Victor E. Smalls

few actually build lasting relationships with it. There is enough money for us all to get rich, they make it every day, our only focus should be how can we make our money make money every day…

The benefits of understanding that money lacks emotion, is that you cause no harm by making money work for you. Making your money work for you is the biggest tool you must master. By mastering this you will set the stage for that lasting relationship with your money. Trust me, having a lasting relationship with money is always a benefit.

When money becomes your employee, that same money becomes a core part of your support system. With money fueling your support system, the opportunities you may be faced with should make more sense now, in relation to the past. Toxic relationships complicate things so much that decisions making becomes a lot harder. These tools are meant to help you build a

The 7 Steps on How To Build A Lasting Relationship With Your Money – Victor E. Smalls

healthy relationship with your money, and once that relationship is maintained, your money will continue to be supportive of your needs.

Money can be loyal to those that treat it right. The main way in which you can treat your money right, is by making sacrifices. You must remove the spending from your life that you enjoy for that moment, but will regret when the gas is low, or the bills need to be paid. This type of spending will be discussed more in chapter four "Needs over Wants". The point needed here is that when you start making sacrifices in life, as it relates to spending, you will see the benefits growing in your bank account. Always keep it in mind, that money has always been loyal to those that take time to understand it.

Establishing a relationship with money is important, but maintaining one is the goal. This relationship as you have read thus far can serve a lot of purpose in your life. It's one of those no brainer

The 7 Steps on How To Build A Lasting Relationship With Your Money – Victor E. Smalls

type of relationships. I push you to become madly in love with your money, and I encourage you to do so by growing with it. As you earn money, sacrifice the things that wouldn't be beneficial to you in the long run. The beautiful thing about sacrificing the things that you don't need, is that it leaves you with more money. This relationship will never let you down, because you are responsible for the way it turns out. Simply put, if you often spend money before you get it, the chances are your relationship will be a toxic one. Now if you take the time to understand money, manage it and commit to growing with it, that commitment will provide more stability, and a stern understanding of your money.

Chapter 2

Save Before You Spend

The 7 Steps on How To Build A Lasting Relationship With Your Money – Victor E. Smalls

"Save Before You Spend"

This is the chapter that will give you and your money the opportunity to really bond, and build that trust you will need to maintain a lasting relationship with it. In this chapter you will learn what saving is, the differences between saving and savings, forms of saving money, the consequences of spending before you save, and why it is important to make saving a habit. "Saving is the key to financial longevity"

The beautiful thing about money is that the more you have, the more you will want to make, however that same drive is what separates most of us from appreciating its worth. The four most common emotions related to spending money is:

1. Sadness
2. Stress
3. Anxiety
4. Happiness

The 7 Steps on How To Build A Lasting Relationship With Your Money – Victor E. Smalls

Recognizing these emotions are important because, they can make your relationships with money end on a sad note, and very fast… I'm pretty sure you have heard someone say, "money is the root to all evils" … That saying can mean many things depending on how you view life. But the most common understanding of it, is greed. Greed is as evil as you allow it to be, when it comes to saving, you can never be too eager to acquire and then save your hard earned money. That type of greed is the best because it can only bring you closer to your money, and trust me we all want to be very close with our money. When I tell you that money talks, believe it! You can have deep conversations with your money, it happens anytime you spend it, save it, or invest it. Money is the best listener; it will do whatever you want. The secret is instructing your money to make more money. When you notice how much your money has grown, your mind starts to wonder more. Following this you will become more inspired to form your own business. Money provides you with the confidence you will need to push forward, rather than walk away from the business

The 7 Steps on How To Build A Lasting Relationship With Your Money – Victor E. Smalls

opportunities. Not only did your money speak to you, it motivated you into thinking about more creative ways to make more money. There is nothing better than creating a way for your hard earned money to become your employee, sounds familiar right.

What Is Saving

Saving is a source of income that is not spent, it is also referred to as deferred consumption. A broader definition is any income not used for immediate consumption. Saving also includes reducing expenditures, such as reoccurring cost. Methods of saving include putting money in, for example, a deposit account, a pension account, an investment fund, or kept in cash. In terms of personal finance, saving generally specifies low risk preservation of money, as in a deposit account, versus investment where risk is a lot higher. Saving does not automatically include interest, but if it can that's what best suits you. Saving differs from savings. When you are saving this refers to an activity occurring over time, like if

The 7 Steps on How To Build A Lasting Relationship With Your Money – Victor E. Smalls

you were someone who wanted to quit smoking cigarettes, and you were used to buying two packs a day, so as part of you going cold turkey you vowed that anytime you get the urge to smoke, you take the cost of the box and saved it, repeating this process over time is saving. Whereas savings refers to something that exist at any one time, like purchasing shares in a stock. This distinction is often misunderstood, but you should have a much clearer view now, right!

Forms of Saving Money

I don't want anyone to become discouraged from investing money, I just want to provide you with information that you may or may not have known, in hopes that you have the best understanding when you decide which ways is best for you to save your money moving forward. The act of saving corresponds to the normal preservation of money for future use. A deposit account paying interest is typically used to hold money for future needs.

The 7 Steps on How To Build A Lasting Relationship With Your Money – Victor E. Smalls

such as a car, house, or even a vacation. This is an effective way to save money, as well as a way to build a personal bond with your money. Treat money right and it will treat you right. I want to make you aware that money used to purchase stocks, placed in an investment fund, or used to buy any asset where there is an element of capital risk, is deemed an investment. This distinction is important as the investment risk can lead to capital loss, unlike cash savings. Cash savings accounts are considered to have minimal risk. In the United States, all banks are required to have deposit insurance, typically issued by the Federal Deposit Insurance Corporation (FDIC). In extreme cases, a bank failure can cause deposits to be lost as it happened at the end of the Great Depression. The FDIC has prevented such things from happening ever since.

Consequences of Spending Before You Save

The 7 Steps on How To Build A Lasting Relationship With Your Money – Victor E. Smalls

The most common act involving money is spending it. The truth is that people are more prone to spending before they save. How many people can you say that you know, spends their entire income tax check months before they get it? They will say things like, I need that 65" smart television, despite the fact that they already have working TV's in each room. Or the ones that enjoy spending in the moment, and later need to borrow money until they get paid? They feel that because they paid for all the drinks that Friday night on payday, and lost track of spending both that night and the days that followed, that now all of a sudden you have to hold them down. Or the one who is a completely different person to deal with when they are without money, rather than when they have it? They rarely want to be bothered, no longer the vibe, but when they get their check it's, "everything is on me". Do you know that some people spend their check within a few days of receiving it? Others spend money just because they have it. Reading this shouldn't make you feel out casted, or even at the center of the joke, because those people I speak of is all of us, not

The 7 Steps on How To Build A Lasting Relationship With Your Money – Victor E. Smalls

just any individual. Yes, we all have room to grow when it comes to financial literacy. That's why it is important for you to master these steps, so you will have the tools needed that will help you build, and maintain a lasting relationship with your money. You will grow to understand that saving will not prevent you from spending, but rather inspire you to become a more responsible spender. You will learn more about Budgeting in Chapter #3, which will touch on the ways on how a healthy budgeting plan can still afford you with the freedom to shop till you drop, you will just do so in a more respectful manner.

Spending is the act of using resources to satisfy current needs and wants. It is seen in contrast to investing, which is spending for acquisition of future income. When you spend, it is vital that each penny spent, that one hundred percent of the appreciated value is demanded. What I'm saying is that you must control your expenditures, the things that you consider to be your necessary expenses, should always be less than or equal to your

The 7 Steps on How To Build A Lasting Relationship With Your Money – Victor E. Smalls

income. A perfect source of income should outweigh your necessary expenses, because this allows you room to save. When your income is equal to your expenses, you're still okay but a side gig may be needed to allow you to at least live a life outside of work and paying bill's.

The consequences of spending before you save can be devastating with marriages, long term relationships, and jobs all feeling the strain. Yes, bad spending habits can affect your personal relationships and your job. The beautiful thing about personal relationships is that you have someone who can reason with you, and plan with you. It's not fair to you or your partner that spending becomes more important than your overall stability together. As for the job, a spender will become more flustered at work because of their spending. Bad spending habits can lead them to be behind on bills, this can create bad energy by that person on non – paydays, affecting other employees on the job, then a false narrative is created in your mind, that the very same job that actually fit a good budgeting plan two months ago when you were

The 7 Steps on How To Build A Lasting Relationship With Your Money – Victor E. Smalls

hired has now become both underpaying and annoying as hell, with a corny manager. That's just crazy but unfortunately it's very true. Bad spending habits has trickle down affects that are often never realized until one hits rock bottom. Other problems can include ruined credit history, or causing one to resort to negative means in which to acquire money, defaulted loans, in some cases bankruptcy, and extreme debt. With all of those financial struggles what likely follows is some form of anxiety, and/or some other stress related mental problems spiraling out of control, leading to physical health issues. All of the above stated can be avoided as it relates to money, so long as you start saving before you spend.

Make Saving a Habit

Once you make saving a habit in your life, you will face a lot less money related stress. Your personal relationships will become more clear, and your financial opportunities will come more frequently. Nothing happens over – night and change from

The 7 Steps on How To Build A Lasting Relationship With Your Money – Victor E. Smalls

your day to day norms can be hard at first, but it's not impossible. The amazing thing about life is that you control your destiny, nobody wants to live a lifetime chasing financial stability, it's on you to go get it done now. Taking the time to save before you spend is your starting point, continuing the pattern will only have a positive financial outcome for you down the line. And that relationship with your money will lead to a marriage, and all you have to do is SAVE, so simple even you can do it.

Chapter 3

Budgeting Your Money

"Budgeting Your Money"

Budgeting is essential for financial stability. This chapter will provide you with simple ways in which you can effectively budget your money. Budgeting helps individuals and families manage their money, prioritize needs, and save for future goals. Once you have mastered this chapter you will have the tools needed for establishing a simple budget based off of an average salary. For the single parent households, this chapter offers insights on how to maintain an effective budget that can meet your unique needs and challenges. Being someone that was raised in a single parent household, I understand how hard it can be to maintain a budget and take care of home. Because of that I felt it was essential to include advice for single parents.

What is Budgeting?

Budgeting is a plan for how you will spend and save your money over a period of time. Although time frames may be different per person, the usual budgeting plan is monthly. The average salary in the United States may vary, so for simplicity, I want you to consider the average household income which is around $70,000 per year as of 2023. For an individual, the average annual salary is around $50,000 per year or about $4,167 per month before taxes. After taxes, this may be reduced to around $3,00 to $3,500, depending on your location, tax filing status, and deductions. To start budgeting effectively, it's essentially to understand your income and how much of it you actually take home.

HERE ARE SOME SIMPLE STEPS FOR CREATING A BUDGET:

a.) Track Your Income and Expenses

The first step in budgeting is tracking all of your sources of income. This could include your salary, bonuses, freelance work, retail income, business income etc. Once you know how much money is coming in each month, you can start tracking your expenses. You should start by categorizing your expenses into fixed and variable expenses.

FIXED EXPENSES

These are the cost that remain the same every month, such as rent/mortgage payments, utilities, car payments, insurance premiums, and subscriptions (e.g., streaming services or maybe WiFi).

VARIABLE EXPENSES

These expenses fluctuate month to month, including groceries, eating out, entertainment, transportation, clothing, and other discretionary spending. Tracking your expenses is vital for identifying areas where you can potentially cut back or make adjustments. Use tools like apps or spreadsheets to keep an eye on your spending habits.

b.) Prioritize Essential Needs

The 7 Steps on How To Build A Lasting Relationship With Your Money – Victor E. Smalls

Before diving head first into budgeting specifics, it's crucial to prioritize essential needs before anything.

MOST ESSENTIAL NEEDS TYPICALLY ARE:

1.) Housing (rent/mortgage)

2.) Utilities (electricity, water, heating)

3.) Food (groceries)

4.) Transportation (car payments, gas, public transportation)

5.) Insurance (health, auto, home etc.)

6.) Debt payments (student loans, bank loans, credit cards)

Once you have these categories covered, you can start working on saving and discretionary spending.

c.) Set Goals

Set short-term and long-term financial goals. Short-term goals may include paying off a credit card or saving for a vacation. Long-term goals could include saving for retirement, buying a home, or building a large emergency fund. Setting clear goals help

The 7 Steps on How To Build A Lasting Relationship With Your Money – Victor E. Smalls

guide your spending decisions and gives you something to work towards.

d.) Choose a Budgeting Method

There are different methods for budgeting that fits different financial situations. Some common ones include the 50/30/20 rule. To be effective using this rule you must set aside 50% of your income for needs, 30% for wants, 20% for savings and debt repayment (10% to save, and 10% for debt repayment). Remember before ant dime is spent, set aside 10% for saving. This method is a simple and effective budgeting system.

e.) Zero Based Budgeting

Every dollar you earn should have a designated purpose, including savings, investment, and expenses. This method will help you better track every cent and ensure that all of your income is distributed effectively.

f.) The Envelope System

This method will help those struggle with overspending, the envelope system is an older approach where you withdraw cash for certain categories (like groceries or entertainment) and can't spend any more in that category for the month.

g.) Cutting Back on Your Unnecessary Expenses

Once you have tracked your income and spending, it's time to look for areas to cut back. Cutting unnecessary expenses can free up more money for saving or paying off debt. Some unnecessary spending can include:

SUBSCRIPTIONS AND MEMBERSHIPS

Cancel subscriptions that you don't use, such as gym memberships, streaming services, etc...

DINING OUT AND TAKEOUT

The 7 Steps on How To Build A Lasting Relationship With Your Money – Victor E. Smalls

Reduce the amount of dining out and prepare meals at home instead, this includes preparing your own coffee. This can significantly limit your grocery bill to the things you need per month, rather than spending daily money on coffee when you already have coffee at home.

SHOPPING AND IMPULSE SPENDING

Avoid impulse purchases by sticking to a shopping list and thinking twice before buying things that aren't necessities. By prioritizing needs and cutting out unnecessary wants, you'll be able to set aside more money toward your savings and long-term goals.

h.) Save and Build an Emergency Fund

One of the most important aspects of budgeting is building an emergency fund. An emergency fund helps you cover unexpected expenses like medical bills, car repairs, or job loss. A good rule of thumb is to have three to six months' worth of living expenses saved up in a high yield account. Start by saving small amounts regularly, automating transfers to your savings account can make this process easier. For instance, you might aim to save 10% of your monthly income. Over time, these savings will have accumulated thus establishing a much needed cushion for unforeseen circumstances.

BUDGETING FOR SINGLE PARENT HOUSEHOLDS

Single parents face unique challenges when it comes to managing their finances. They are often responsible for providing for families on just one income while balancing childcare, education, and other responsibilities. Proper budgeting is crucial for single parents to ensure financial stability, and meet the needs of their children. Also take note that the parent is the child's first teacher, and idol, as such the way you handle money will likely be mimicked by your children in one way or another, so maintaining a lasting relationship with your money is very important.

TRACK BOTH PERSONAL AND CHILD RELATED EXPENSES

In addition to regular household expenses, single parent's must consider expenses related to raising children, including childcare, school supplies, clothing, extracurricular activities, and health care. Start by tracking all the cost associated with raising your children and ensure that these expenses are factored into your overall budget. Also it is important to live well within your means, your income should be about two thirds higher that your monthly expenses. This only means that you have to cut back on more than the average individual to be effective in your budgeting plan. Child related expenses could be categorized as follows:

Childcare or School Fees

a.) Medical and Dental Expenses

b.) Clothing

c.) Extracurricular Activities (sports, camp)

d.) Transportation (school pick-up, after school programs)

These expenses are essential, so it's important to prioritize them accordingly.

LEVERAGE ASSISTANCE PROGRAMS AND BENEFITS

Single parents often qualify for various forms of government assistance or local programs. Utilize these as ways to limit the amount of money you'll need to dish out each month on expenses. Obviously this accounts for those single parents who are on government assistance. When you work and are on government assistance you add the money you get from the government funding as total income then establish your budgeting from there. Understanding what financial assistance programs you have and taking advantage of them can help reduce the burden on your budget.

CREATE A FAMILY FRIENDLY BUDGET

When creating a budgeting plan, consider how you can make it work for you and your children. A family friendly budget

The 7 Steps on How To Build A Lasting Relationship With Your Money – Victor E. Smalls

should take into account your personal expenses and the additional costs of raising a family. Here are some strategies:

Plan meals in advance to avoid impulse spending and make the most of your grocery budget. Use coupons and discounts for clothing, food, and other child related needs. Many stores offer loyalty programs or discounts for parents. It is important to keep all receipts, the money that you spend that is taxed, **IS MONEY OWED TO YOU COME TAX SEASON…**

Some other things to make habits of doing when saving is to set aside a portion of your income for your children's education (such as college savings account) and for emergency savings. It's also helpful to involve your children in budgeting discussions when they are old enough. Teaching them about money management can foster financial responsibility in the long run. In addition to day to day budgeting, single parents must also think about long-term financial goals and strategies for building wealth.

The 7 Steps on How To Build A Lasting Relationship With Your Money – Victor E. Smalls

Working towards financial independence is key for single parents because in time you build the needed confidence to not just build a lasting relationship with your money, but you also maintain it. As a single parent it is very important to plan for retirement. Although it may seem like a distant concern, the earlier you start saving, the more you will benefit from in compound interest. If you have access to a 401(k) through your employer, try to contribute enough to take advantage of any employer match. Additionally, consider setting up an Individual Retirement Account (IRA) to further grow your savings.

A great way to create a college fund for your children is by setting up 529 College Savings Plan. This type of account allows your money to grow tax free and can be used to pay for qualified education expenses. The secret is to start saving early, even if it's only a small amount each month, as the saving can help reduce the financial burden of higher education in the future. Investing for long-term growth is always important when you are a single parent.

The 7 Steps on How To Build A Lasting Relationship With Your Money – Victor E. Smalls

When you begin saving consistently, consider investing some of your savings into stocks, bonds, or mutual funds. Investments can help build wealth over time, providing a potential income stream beyond your salary. However, investing comes with risks, so it's important to educate yourself or consult a financial advisor before taking this step.

Budgeting on an average salary, especially for single parents, can be challenging, but it's entirely possible with the right strategies in place. By carefully tracking your income and expenses, prioritizing essential needs, cutting unnecessary spending, and saving for the future, you can and will build financial stability and achieve your long-term goals. Remember, budgeting is an ongoing process. It requires flexibility and regular evaluation to ensure that you are staying on track. For single parents, this may mean adjusting to unexpected expenses or finding creative ways to stretch your budget further.

However, with perseverance and a clear plan, you can and will create a secure future for both you and your children. By

The 7 Steps on How To Build A Lasting Relationship With Your Money – Victor E. Smalls

building a foundation of financial literacy and discipline, you can work towards a stable and prosperous financial future, regardless of your class level.

Chapter 4

Avoiding a Fixed-Mindset Vs. Becoming One with the Growth-Mindset

"Avoiding the Fixed-Mindset

VS.

Becoming One with the Growth-Mindset"

Avoiding a fixed-mindset is the key maintaining a lasting relationship with your money. This chapter will help you become aware of the traits related to a fixed-mindset, and how to overcome them.

Having a fixed-mindset can close your mind in ways that will alter your ability to grow. The one positive result that comes from having a fixed-mindset is that you become aware of the negatives that deal with such a mindset. The most common traits people experience when having a fixed-mindset is:

1. Avoids Challenges
2. Shy away from things they don't know
3. Unable to handle feedback

4. Intelligence and talent lacks development
5. Do not carry out any actions without first seeking approval
6. Threatened by the success of others
7. Effort is not regarded as being fruitful
8. Understanding failure as the limit of ability
9. Gives up easily

Confidence in self and the will to grow is what it takes to overcome the fixed-mindset. Those of you who say things like, I can't do this because, or I'm not going to because, I say to you, why not try… It is best to do all in your power to avoid a fixed-mindset, if you are fixed on something it can become an issue at some point, especially when dealing with money. For example, if you're fixed on a weekend out with friends early in the month, you're more likely to overspend thus creating an issue with bills come month's end. Instead your fixation should be what's coming down the line that you should be planning for right now, and what changes must you make in your own budget to get you and your money where you need to be. By doing this, you are setting necessary goals that will strengthen the bond between you and your money, and bring you mush closer to having a growth-mindset.

GROWTH-MINDSET

Becoming one with a growth-mindset will take you to the next level in life, both as a person, and as it relates to your overall outlook about money. One secret to remember is that, "although awareness of a fixed-mindset is the key to success, becoming one with the growth-mindset opens the door to overall success". When you are navigating through life with a growth-mindset, you view challenges differently, they now become opportunities, you become more willing and open to acknowledge and embrace your weaknesses, and learn to both give and receive constructive criticism. This is the mindset to have when you're determined to maintain a lasting relationship with your money. A growth-mindset breeds a mental strength, and allows you to become more disciplined with your money. For example, you will become more

The 7 Steps on How To Build A Lasting Relationship With Your Money – Victor E. Smalls

in tune with living on less than you earn, or open to learning more ways to make what you earn work for you.

A growth-mindset allows your intelligence and talents to become more dynamic over time. While a person with a fixed-mindset will seek approval from someone before moving forward with their visions, a person with a growth-mindset will prioritize learning and mastering their craft, and following through without seeking approval. Once you have developed a routine to focus more on the process, instead of the end result, you will begin to understand the true value in your hard work and effort. A growth-mindset makes you elite, so as an elitist, you should NEVER HATE on the next person's success. Even if you don't like this person or understand their ways and/or walks of life, find a civilized way to support them. Elitist must be inspired by the success of others, and become motivated into being the NEXT inspirational success story. In order for you to truly become one with the growth-mindset, you must learn and understand that failure is nothing more than an opportunity to grow. So please remain persistent in the face of setbacks…

The 7 Steps on How To Build A Lasting Relationship With Your Money – Victor E. Smalls

An individual's mindset affects the motivation to practice and learn. People with a fixed-mindset believe that little can be done to improve ability. Feedback is seen as their underlining ability and success is seen as a result of this ability, not any effort expended. Constructive criticism from an advisor is often challenged, limiting the learning point from ever surfacing. Failure is intimidating, since it would suggest limiting things they would not be able to overcome. Those with a fixed-mindset tend to avoid challenges, give up easily, and focus on the outcome. They have this belief that their abilities are fixed, and any effort has little to no value.

Those with a growth-mindset believe that intellect can be developed, and their abilities can be increased through learning and application. They are likely to take on challenges, preserve when faced with adversity, they have no issue with accepting and learning from failure, will always focus on the process rather than the outcome, and see abilities as skills which are developed through effort. Constructive criticism and failure are seen as opportunities to increase their ability, signaling the need to focus, put forth effort, apply time to practice, and master the learning opportunity.

Now that you understand how a fixed-mindset and a growth-mindset affects the ways you deal with your money, there should only be one mindset worth moving forward with. The problem with that is, that in life we are often faced with both. When you look at it, both mindsets work hand in hand, "most success stories arise from failure". The only question left to ask is; How long do you want to have a fixed-mindset? Do you consider yourself to be an elite?

I encourage you to start today, put your thinking cap on and get to work. Make sure that everything you do from this day forward is linked to your growth-mindset. I believe in you! Do you believe in yourself? I trust that you do believe in yourself, because you took the time out of your day to read this book. That in itself is a sign of you already connecting with a growth-mindset, by willing yourself to learn. Now it's time to take action, put what you've learned to work, and be great in all that you do…

Chapter 5

Invest Into Your Own Visions

The 7 Steps on How To Build A Lasting Relationship With Your Money – Victor E. Smalls

"Invest Into Your Own Visions"

Investing into your own visions is an essential element you must master while building a lasting relationship with your money. After reading this chapter you will be more focused and determined to take the next step in chasing your dream. The issues many of us have, is that we often overlook our own visions. The problem with overlooking your visions is that you lose out on golden opportunities.

As stated before I believe in YOU, the goal is to get you to believe in yourself. A wise man once said to me that, "you miss 100% of the shots you don't take". At first I saw this as a basketball related metaphor, and allowed it to go in one ear and out the other. Years later I replayed the entire conversation while in deep thought, and realized just how valuable that advice was. We allow our own thoughts or the thoughts of jealous individuals to sway us into abandoning our visions. I want you to change your way of thinking and really take the time to understand how your vision can become a cash cow.

The 7 Steps on How To Build A Lasting Relationship With Your Money – Victor E. Smalls

The biggest mistake that we make is that we can't wait to tell someone what our visions are. You don't need approval from anyone but yourself! Once you allow the next person to dictate the moves you make, you've already failed. That's not to say that everyone is "Debby Downers", there are many elites out there who have encouraging advice, and are even willing to invest into your visions.

In no way should you to be discouraged whenever you decide to build with a friend about your visions. The key to gaining the most out of your conversation is by building with the right friend. You know your circle better than, anyone, as you know the ones who have common sense and the ones who are stuck in their ways. Find the ones who understand what you're talking about, and who are willing to hold that level of conversation. Food for thought, "the biggest way to destroy a big dream is to introduce that dream to a small mind".

I have a simple process that you and a few like-minded associates within your circle can consider, it is called an

The 7 Steps on How To Build A Lasting Relationship With Your Money – Victor E. Smalls

INVESTMENT CLUB. A simple way to actually create an effective investment club is by getting together with about four like-minded associates (smaller groups tend to yield the best results). The next step is to figure out a reasonable amount of money each of you can initially bring to the table like $250 (=$1,000), then each month you all put about $50 each (=$200) to the original pot monthly. In just one year that original $1,000 that was brought to the table collectively turned into $3,400. Just like that your team has capital, now it's time to sit at the table and allow each person to express a vision that they believe can become a formidable business. The key to an investment club being successful is that you set an initial goal or pact that everybody's vision will become a functioning business, while creating a positive environment that promotes prosperity and undeniable success. An investment club is a safe way to invest into your own dreams.

Another way to remain determined while investing into your own visions is by taking time to educate yourself. When you

The 7 Steps on How To Build A Lasting Relationship With Your Money – Victor E. Smalls

have a vision but lack the needed knowledge required to piece it all together, you must take time to gain some understanding. For example, you may not know how to start a LLC, so you may find it helpful to google this or look it up on YouTube. You can only gain from this education. Remember, when you take time to educate yourself, you have effectively taken the first step into mastering your visions. Pursuing your own visions requires time and dedication as such you must get accustomed to note taking. Really use this time to understand whatever it is you're being taught. Don't get lazy and pick a time out the day where you know you'll be tired. Find a time where you're up and prepared to take your visions to the next level. None of this requires you to spend a dollar, most of this knowledge is FREE. Just knowing that you can began to master your visions for free is amazing. It's about taking advantage of every opportunity you are presented with, and in the midst of adversity you must always find the simplest ways to overcome it

My principles to investing in yourself are:

The 7 Steps on How To Build A Lasting Relationship With Your Money – Victor E. Smalls

1. Take your visions serious
2. Believe in YOU all the time
3. Never allow the next person to dictate your push
4. Seek like-minded associates
5. Educate yourself
6. Master your craft
7. Recognize the positives that comes from failure

These principles can guide you in a positive direction whenever you have an idea that you truly believe in. As humans we sometimes become our own worst enemy, the harsh reality is that we are all born winners. Just look at the odds you've beat just to be in existence. During conception it was a race to be where you are right now, and the fact that you're reading this means you were one of the lucky ones. Just knowing that should inspire you each day into being the best version of yourself. Trust in your visions, believe in your abilities, and never think any of your goals are out of reach. Be great in all that you do, continue to beat the odds, and see past the naysayers. You only have one life to live, why not live

The 7 Steps on How To Build A Lasting Relationship With Your Money – Victor E. Smalls

it to your fullest potential. It starts by investing into your own visions. **GET TO WORK!!!**

Chapter 6

Prioritizing Needs Over Wants

The 7 Steps on How To Build A Lasting Relationship With Your Money – Victor E. Smalls

"Prioritizing Needs Over Wants"

This chapter is meant to make you aware of the pitfalls that comes with unnecessary spending over responsible spending. You will also learn about playing the long game when dealing with finances, and how you can obtain all the things that you want in due time. Money works for all those that work to maintain it.

A key factor in maintaining a lasting relationship with your money effectively is by understanding the differences between needs and wants. When you learn to refrain from unnecessary spending on the things that you want, and focus on those more important things that you may need. I can assure you that your savings will grow, and in the long run you will be able to acquire the things that you want without overstepping your budget. Prioritizing is nothing more than a mindset shift, it shows that you are conscious about the things you do before you do them.

The 7 Steps on How To Build A Lasting Relationship With Your Money – Victor E. Smalls

THE DIFFERNCES BETWEEN NEEDS AND WANTS

A need is something you can't go without it is the most important thing you will spend your money on. For example, if you have a flat tire and need a repair, it would be smart to spend money to get it fixed. The benefit of getting it fixed is that your car will help you get to and from work on time. Getting to and from work allows for you to make more money than what was spent on the repair in the first place. That tire example was meant to show you how spending on a need can help you more in the long run. In every single parent household bills and food are amongst the first of which money will be spent on. When you are managing your expenses this is called being stable. Although being stable shows responsibility, it alone does not transition into financial stability. This comes when you understand that every purchase you make must produce a return in the long run. Paying your bills provides shelter for you and your family, buying food allows nourishment, spending money on affordable clothes helps with our appearance

The 7 Steps on How To Build A Lasting Relationship With Your Money – Victor E. Smalls

and more work opportunities. A need is something that will benefit you in return, the term often used is, "money well spent".

A want is often referred to something one desires to have. We often fall victim to purchasing wants without maintaining a healthy budget. It's the classic spending money you don't really have, or living beyond your means. Wants can become a liability if your spending habits are without reason. Some people simply spend money on a pair of sneakers because they see everyone else doing it, as with other things. The whole "monkey see monkey do" theory is a reality to a lot of people, and it causes unnecessary spending to occur without reason. When people have cash on hand, and they see something they like they buy it not thinking about how this purchase will affect them when it comes time to pay bills.

One example you can consider is that if you make $3,500 a month and your rent is $1,800, your other bills total out to $1,100. That leaves you with a $600 a month budget. If you go buy a pair of expensive shoes and an outfit to go with it during your first paycheck totaling $800 well you are now $200 in the hole before

The 7 Steps on How To Build A Lasting Relationship With Your Money – Victor E. Smalls

you even paid one bill, or even saved a dime. Although you may look fly for a day, you will suffer by the end of the month. Just because you have a $600 monthly budget does not mean you can spend it all on the things you desire. It's one thing if you'd find a similar outfit and shoes for around $200, at least you're left with $400 in your budget for the month. Getting comfortable with spending money on wants is not a recipe for success, to play the long game you want to survive on less in the short run, while saving more and have more in the long run. It's common knowledge that by maintaining a lasting relationship with your money, you will be able to purchase the things you desire and want the most. The goal is to prioritize more on the things that are most important and will produce a return down the line.

One way to prioritize more effectively is by learning to budget, this called **ROLL OVER MONEY:**

Roll over money is money that you have left over from your budget that rolls into the next month. Now with roll over money you can do one or two things. (1) you can add the roll over

The 7 Steps on How To Build A Lasting Relationship With Your Money – Victor E. Smalls

money to your savings (2) you can use it to have a bigger budget in the next month. The thing about that is that it gives you more wiggle room when you choose to spend. This is especially effective when getting close to the end of summer and school supplies are needed for the kids, now you can get a little extra stuff without hurting your August budget. Roll over money is what's most encouraged because it will become addictive and once you have an addiction it takes far more convincing to switch your ways. But ask yourself; Who wouldn't want to save more money while living well within their means? It's a no brainer, save money now so in the long run you can enjoy more, **BE ELITE**...

In order for you to get accustomed to shifting your mind towards prioritizing needs over wants, you have to focus on the things that are most important in your life. Once you apply this way of thinking to your daily activities, your priorities will become far more relevant and every dollar you spend will not have a negative effect on you later on down the line. Financial literacy is only effective when the one applying it buys into its philosophy. I

The 7 Steps on How To Build A Lasting Relationship With Your Money – Victor E. Smalls

have faith in you, do what you need to do in order to take full advantage of the money you earn… **BE ELITE!**

Chapter 7

Reaping the Benefits of Your Money in the Long Run

The 7 Steps on How To Build A Lasting Relationship With Your Money – Victor E. Smalls

"Reaping the Benefits of Your Money in the Long Run"

The benefits from sound financial management come when you commit to saving, budgeting, and investing wisely. Remember that you lay the foundation for a secure financial future. The key to reaping the long term rewards of your money is patience and consistency. Compound interest, for example, is a powerful tool that allows your investment to grow over time.

In addition to traditional savings and investment options like stocks, bonds, and retirement accounts. Consider diversifying your investments to include real estate other passive income streams. Building wealth takes time, but with discipline and focus, your efforts will produce financial benefits that provides security, freedom, and peace of mind in the future.

By following the seven steps provided below you will take control of your financial future and achieve the financial freedom that you desire:

The 7 Steps on How To Build A Lasting Relationship With Your Money – Victor E. Smalls

1. Understanding your money
2. Save before you spend
3. Budgeting
4. Avoiding the fixed-mindset
5. Invest into your own visions
6. Prioritizing needs over wants
7. Reaping the benefits of your money in the long run

Mastering money management requires commitment, but the rewards are worth the effort. With a clear plan, and a thoughtful mindset, you can create the financial life you've always dreamed of.

WORDS OF MOTIVATION

Mastering money management is a powerful tool in life. It enables us to: meet our needs, pursue our desires, and build a future for ourselves and our families. However, the way we manage our money significantly impacts our ability to achieve financial freedom and security. Mastering money management involves understanding your finances, making sound decisions about your spending and saving, and investing in your future. This process requires discipline, education, and a shift in mindset. By following the seven steps that this book provides, you will develop a strong financial foundation that will ultimately lead to long term success… **I BELIEVE IN YOU AND YOU CAN DO IT! IT'S RIGHT AT YOUR FINGERTIPS, IT'S NEVER TOO LATE TO START. LETS GET IT!!!!**

WISE WORDS FROM A GOOD BROTHER

"The relationship you have with your finances, is the same as any relationship shared with a friend, lover, or spouse. It's a bond created by chemistry. The way you treat this bond, will dictate the health of that relationship"

By: Mr. C. Bennett

www.ingramcontent.com/pod-product-compliance
Lightning Source LLC
Chambersburg PA
CBHW052206070526
44585CB00017B/2092